We Can Fix It!

How to disrupt the impact of Big Money on politics

Nelson Morgan

With a foreword by George Lakoff

With many contributions from Antonia Scatton, Julia Bernd, Madelaine Plauché, and Barath Raghavan

and

Art by Clay Butler

Foreword

All politics is moral, and voters vote for what they see is right. It is important that politicians understand this, and focus on connecting to the voters' values. These are themes I've written about extensively.

It turns out that there are tangible positive effects of doing this that might not be immediately apparent. While research has shown that a positive, values-based approach to electioneering is far more likely to be successful than one based on attack ads or attempts to focus on the undesirability of your opponent's ideas, it also has the potential to promote democratic principles, when implemented by training ordinary citizens who want to be spokespeople to speak out in their communities.

And, to the point raised in this little book, such methods have the potential to reduce the importance of (and dependence on) the mad scramble for huge sums that is a standard part of large political campaigns.

The campaign strategies currently in place have led to the current expensive infrastructure. It is time to look closely at these strategies and question them. This booklet is about a piece of this new outlook, the part that is a way out of the dominance of the effect of large campaign contributions.

George Lakoff

Berkeley, 2016

Preface

A tsunami of money has flooded the American political landscape in recent years. Many commentators have discussed its corrosive effect, which has worsened since the Supreme Court's Citizens United decision, but attempts to address the problem have been insufficient. Some concerned individuals and groups have proposed to reduce the supply of campaign funds (for example, by constitutional amendment), or to focus on transparency in the hope that sunlight will shame those who are giving and accepting huge quantities of cash.

There is a different approach that has been overlooked: instead of focusing on transparency or the supply of money in politics, we can focus on the demand side of the equation. Our group, UpRise Campaigns, has been working on reducing the demand for large contributions by using new approaches to simultaneously lower costs and increase the effectiveness of campaigns. In short, we aim to make a low-cost campaign more effective than a big-money campaign, reducing the necessity for big-money donors and thereby minimizing their influence.

The key challenge for our work is how to provide campaigns with what they need to win, even if they don't have deep pockets. Big-budget campaigns hire political consultants who manage the campaign's war chest, spending a large proportion of the funds on advertising, and in particular on TV ads. We think it is possible to deliver a candidate's message more effectively and far more cheaply – and in the process, to refocus the campaign on people, not money.

Our project aims to build systems and community training

methods to leverage the unique skills, relationships, and creativity that motivated citizens can contribute, and to help them become the heart of political campaigns.

Leveraging citizen power in campaigns is not a new idea; ordinary, passionate campaign volunteers have been the most powerful advocates for many campaigns, as their authenticity and relationships cannot be matched by advertising. However, few campaigns have been able to leverage citizen volunteers effectively at scale. The main challenge is how to empower volunteers and take advantage of their potentially invaluable contributions, while at the same time mitigating the chaos that can ensue when trying to coordinate thousands or millions of people.

This little book suggests a first step toward overcoming this false dichotomy: directly empower citizens to contribute to campaigns by giving them (and the campaigns) a system that enables them to effectively coordinate, communicate, and manage their activities. One key to this is the automated matching of volunteer skills with a campaign's needs, focusing on the physical world the campaign inhabits – ensuring that each campaign need, each event, each idea can be automatically matched with volunteers who have skills, relationships, or other resources at their disposal to help make it happen. Such a system would match the needs involved in a local campaign event (e.g., a presentation to a community group) with people who have relevant experience (e.g., public speaking) or equipment (e.g., a projector), or have relationships that can increase the impact of the event (e.g., personal connections with the community group in question). A new candidate might need a graphic designer, a t-shirt shop or a place that can print bumper stickers, and lots of people to distribute them.

Automating this aspect can help tame the complexity inherent in a large campaign, and can allow each citizen volunteer to do what they do best on behalf of that campaign. In this way, a campaign with little money can scale up its citizen force in order to dominate the political landscape and conversation, reaching potential voters in a much more effective manner than advertising. And in the process, volunteers can feel more valued, and will be more motivated to participate in future campaigns.

Democracy at its core is a human-to-human endeavor – something that has been lost in our modern political era. We believe that our approach of introducing this new technology will actually help re-humanize and re-democratize what has become a costly, mechanized, and corrupt political system.

Contents

Part I: The Problem

Houston, we have a problem.
– Apollo 13 mission, 1970 (as rephrased by Hollywood)

1. The status quo

Our entire political process has been corrupted by a flood of money.

U.S. Presidential Campaigns, Total Cost in Millions

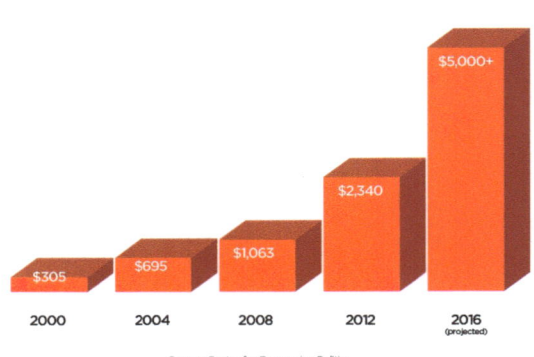

Source: Center for Responsive Politics

The cost of campaigning is escalating out of control, nearly *doubling* every presidential election.

Candidates have to spend more than **8 hours a day raising money**. Once in office, they still have to spend **4-8 hours a day** raising money. They have little time left to interact with voters or do their jobs!

Since the Supreme Court's **Citizens United** ruling on expenditures made by groups outside of official campaigns, the campaign process has been flooded with donations from corporations and wealthy individuals through unlimited Super PACs and untraceable "dark money".

It has never been easier to buy influence, and the results show when groups like the NRA can get Congress to vote against gun background checks,

2

despite terrorist attacks, an epidemic of mass shootings, and 88% bi-partisan support from the American public.

Sen. @ThomTillis received $2,459,881 in expenditures from NRA. He voted against today's background check measure

2. How we got here

It's not just Citizens United...

The landmark Citizens United Supreme Court decision in 2010 (in the case of Citizens United v. Federal Election Commission) opened up the doors to contributions from corporations to organizations that were (supposedly) independent of political campaigns. In that decision, the conservative majority stated "this Court now concludes that independent expenditures, including those made by corporations, do not give rise to corruption or the appearance of corruption." It was an endorsement of the idea that only quid pro quo corruption, that is, the direct exchange of money for an official act, would count as corruption.

In fact, what followed was an unprecedented rise in expenditures outside of campaigns per se. In particular, the ruling fueled a rise in the class of not-for-profit organizations in the 501(c)(4) tax category. These entities are supposed to exist for the public good, but often are (or become) shadow organizations that feed dark money (money whose origin is disguised) to Super PACs, which then spend huge sums for political purposes. While contribution limits still exist for campaigns per se, wealthy donors (including corporations) can provide unlimited sums to a Super PAC to attack particular candidates, in order to further the donor's agenda.

But this decision and its consequences were not the origin of this problem; rather, they were just the next chapter in the history of big money's influence on our electoral process. Concerns about campaign finance are also not new; these issues led to legislation and court actions in the 1970s. For instance, in 1971, Congress passed the Federal Election Campaign Act (FECA), which increased the transparency of contributions for candidates at the federal level, and also limited campaign contributions to candidates as well as campaign-related spending. The Supreme Court heard a challenge to FECA's constitutionality 5 years later (Buckley v. Valeo), and rendered a mixed decision – donation limits were (for the most part) upheld, but the spending caps were not. Additionally, this decision limited disclosure requirements for contributions, and the limits on independent expenditures (for instance, money spent by an independent group to run ads favoring a candidate) were ruled unconstitutional based on a "free speech" argument.

Later legislation and several key Supreme Court rulings also weighed in on this issue before Citizens United. For instance, in 2002, Congress passed legislation to reform campaign finance with the Bipartisan Campaign Reform Act (BCRA), also known as "McCain-Feingold", reflecting the bipartisan sponsorship of the bill. This bill added constraints on so-called "soft money" that could come from political parties or from corporate or union sources. As usual, the law was challenged in court (in McConnell v. Federal Election Commission), but most of the provisions were upheld. However, the decision did not affect the ability of non-profit organizations to contribute to campaigns, and the bill itself left out regulation of certain types of non-profits (so-called "527" organizations, named for a tax code section), which do not fall under FEC jurisdiction so long as they don't coordinate with campaigns.

These (and other) prior actions by Congress and the courts reflect concern about campaign finance and reactions to abuses, leading up to the Citizens United decision. But that latter decision opened up another potential floodgate of money, by striking down any limits at all on election spending by organizations that accepted union or corporate funds, again with the rationale of preserving the right to freedom of speech. This was just the latest defeat in the four-decade fight to fix campaign finance.

It's fun to talk about billionaires throwing bags of money on a politician's desk, but that's not how it works (at least for the campaigns proper). Our elected representatives (and those aspiring to that role) have to beg for it. Wealthy donors have many people asking for their support – and people who have $2700 to put into multiple campaigns are not the majority of Americans. This means that candidates need to spend a major part of their time and energy contacting potential donors and trying to get their money.

Representative Steve Israel, the former head of the Democratic Congressional Campaign Committee (DCCC), noted in a *New York Times* op-ed piece[1], after describing the ideals with which he went to Congress, hoping to spend his time changing the country for the better:

"The money race began, and I attended political action committee fund-raisers, which are like panhandling with hors d'oeuvres. There were hours

[1] January 8, 2016:
http://www.nytimes.com/2016/01/09/opinion/steve-israel-confessions-of-a-congressman.html?smid=fb-share&_r=0

of 'call time' – huddled in a cubicle, dialing donors.
Sometimes double dialing and triple dialing.
Whispering sweet nothings and other small talk into
the phone in hopes of receiving large somethings.
I'd sit next to an assistant who collated 'call sheets'
with donor's names, contribution histories, and
other useful information. ('How's Sheila? Your
wife. Oh, Shelly? Sorry.') Since then, I've spent
roughly 4,200 hours in call time, attended more
than 1,600 fund-raisers just for my own campaign,
and raised nearly $20 million in increments of
$1,000, $2,500, and $5,000 per election cycle."

So politicians are significantly distracted from policy questions, and meanwhile dark money can enable huge expenditures that would not be possible within the campaigns.

But let's ask a more basic question: why is it so expensive to run? As of 2012, the average cost of a run for a U.S. House seat is $1.7 million, and for a Senate seat, $10 million. And for the national presidential campaign, it can be hundreds of millions of dollars.[2]

Where does the money go?

---

[2] As of May 2016, some estimates for the year's presidential campaign costs reach over a billion dollars per party.

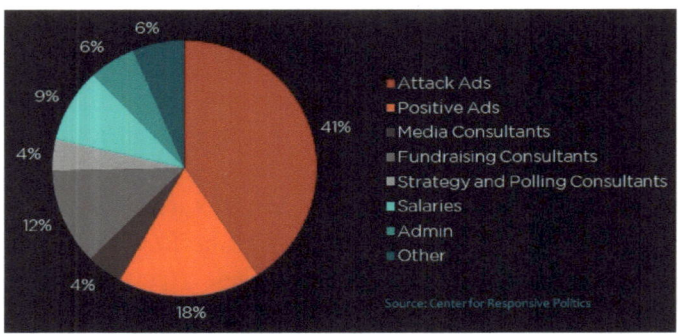

According to the Center for Responsive Politics, 79% of a typical (large) campaign budget goes to advertising and consultants.

'Twas not always thus. In his 1948 presidential campaign, Harry S. Truman was reportedly proud to have shaken approximately 500,000 hands and traveled 31,000 miles across the nation. Television was a novelty that few had access to. Eisenhower's campaign in 1952 incorporated commercials, but it was really the 1960 Kennedy-Nixon campaign that demonstrated the importance of television, and the sweaty demeanor that Nixon presented may have been a key factor in his defeat. And it was the 1964 "Daisy" ad[3], suggesting that a vote for Goldwater was a vote for nuclear destruction, that really convinced many of the power of TV advertisements – although it ran only once as an ad per se, and its impact was largely felt through news coverage and public outcry. (However, the evidence is not actually definitive that it was a deciding factor in that race.)

---

[3] "Daisy", Sid Myers, Aaron Ehrlich, Stan Lee, and Gene Case (Doyle Dan Bernbach Ad Agency) and Tony Schwartz, 1964, available at
https://www.youtube.com/watch?v=dDTBnsqxZ3k.

From that point on, with each election, the body of consultants schooled in media presentations grew. And as the figure in the "status quo" section at the start of Part I shows, in the 21st century, the costs have gone off the charts.

So here we are now: corporations and other major sponsors know that they must play the game in order to have influence, and politicians know that they must play too or they will be swamped by the other side. And candidates know that they have to start fundraising for the next election cycle just days after they win an election.

It's a merry-go-round, and no one knows how to get off.

3. Consequences

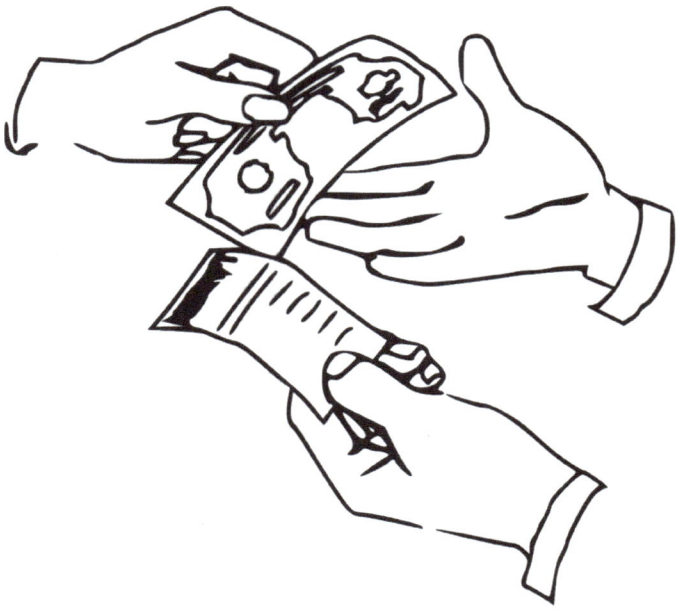

It really matters how our electoral system functions.

It is an oft-cited truism that "elections have consequences." When one side or the other gets elected, they have some power to implement their agenda – though often not as much as one would think.

But the electoral system itself has consequences too. While quid pro quo corruption via the direct exchange of money for votes is relatively rare, subtler corruption is rife. Legislators moderate their positions to avoid alienating donors and classes of donors. Even candidates who honestly support the positions of major donors are more likely to gain traction because of that support, leaving other potential candidates unable to seriously compete, even if they hold positions that are popular with the public. "I don't care who does the electing, so long as I get to do the nominating" is a quote attributed to Boss Tweed, who ran machine politics in New York in the mid-19th century. It seems appropriate for the current phenomenon. The main difference is that the U.S. as a whole is much more complex than 19th century New York City, and there is not any one person or group who entirely controls the choice of candidates.

But indirect corruption is not the only consequence of this system. An even subtler one, alluded to earlier in this little book, is the domination of legislators' time by fundraising. How much does this matter?

It matters a lot!

Have you ever gone to Congress and sat in one of the galleries (House or Senate)? It's not as interesting as it used to be… Typically, there is one Representative or Senator there, talking to the camera. Where are the others? Making phone calls for donations! Or on their way to a fundraiser, or… They often only spend 3 days a week in Congress at all. There is little if any time for socializing with their colleagues, which in the past had a significant role in facilitating compromise; and the time and capacity for actually working through their differences is minimized, as noted in the earlier Steve Israel quote.

So they hold their positions, show up for some committee meetings, and make little progress on actual governing. In many cases, the actual legislation is written by lobbyists, and the legislators have little time for studying it. And as described beautifully in a video from represent.us[4], campaign contributions from large financial interests make it unlikely that our elected representatives will pass regulatory legislation that the public hugely supports.

The confluence of the impact of big donors and the dominance of fundraising in how legislators spend their days has meant that progress on some of the major issues of our time (e.g., financial regulation, immigration, gun control) has slowed to a crawl.[5]

4

https://www.youtube.com/watch?list=PLKePI0ZbnT69klhhd
VXnd9-eFdx5iIh5W&v=5tu32CCA_Ig

[5] There are, of course, other factors that have led to the recent gridlock – the effects of the Great Recession of 2008, the rise of the Tea Party, etc. But we maintain that the direct and indirect effects of the campaign finance merry-go-round are a key factor in the slowing of progress.

Part II. Current Attempts at Reform

You can't fix a bad script after you start shooting. The problems on the page only get bigger as they move to the big screen.
– Howard Hawks

1. Transparency

We need to know who's giving what money to what politician.

One important approach to reducing the influence of big money on politics is to press for transparency about contributions. This should be required in a free society – we should do away with hidden deals of the kind that can influence public policy. If our politicians are to be accountable to the public, contributions should be in the public record. And voters can make more informed decisions about legislators who support or oppose a bill regarding prescription medicine, for instance, if they see that those legislators were heavily funded by pharmaceutical companies.

There are a number of organizations working for transparency. The Center for Responsive Politics (www.opensecrets.org) provides extremely useful information about money's role in U.S. politics, both for electoral campaigns and for lobbying. The

Sunlight Foundation (sunlightfoundation.com) also advocates for greater transparency about the currently unregulated dark money in our elections. In fact, they do more than publicize the money flow; both organizations are part of an effort to make information about a variety of aspects of government and elections much more accessible to the general public.

MapLight (maplight.org) focuses specifically on the influence of money in politics, by not only tracking the contributions, but how the politicians receiving the money vote on bills. Another organization, the National Institute on Money in State Politics (www.followthemoney.org) provides an archive of contributions to political campaigns in all 50 states. They compile information about campaign donors, lobbyists, and more in a way that is much easier to access than by poring through government records.

We believe that these efforts towards transparency are vital, though, by themselves, they are not sufficient. To begin with, although an industrious and curious voter or journalist can benefit greatly from the improved access to campaign finance information, the vast majority of voters will never connect the dots, even with these tools. And, as noted earlier, since the Citizens United Supreme Court decision of 2010, unlimited contributions can be made anonymously to 501(c)(4) organizations (such as Karl Rove's "Crossroads GPS"), and those funds can in turn be donated to Super PACs – who then can finance huge ad campaigns. But the progress that has been made on transparency is something that we can build on, augmenting these efforts with other approaches.

In short, efforts to make political contributions transparent are necessary, but not sufficient to significantly disrupt the influence of big money on politics. So, what about changing the law?

2. Legislation

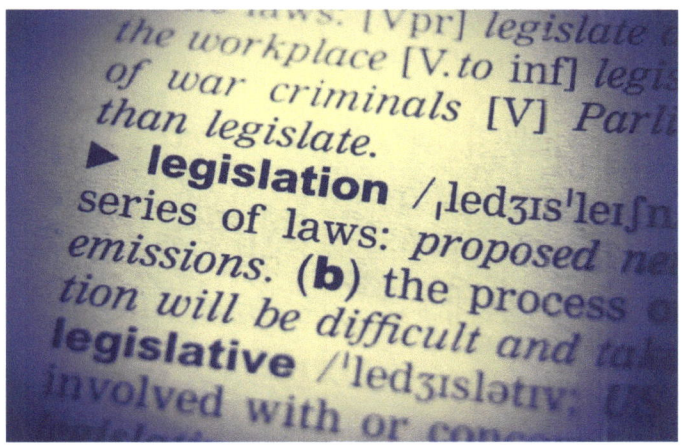

We need laws that protect our democracy.

* U.S. federal laws

Over the years, a number of federal laws have been passed to restrict campaign contributions (e.g., McCain-Feingold/BCRA, which in 2002 updated the Federal Election Campaign Act of 1971). In each case, work-arounds were developed by powerful interest groups, enabling them to promote their causes and candidates with large amounts of money.

Because of these work-arounds and direct attacks like Citizens United, there are significant limitations on what Congress can do to address the problem of the influence of big money on our electoral process. Additionally, many members of Congress themselves are addicted to the status quo – their concern over their ability to get re-elected can often trump any concern over the implicit corruption, or even their weariness with constantly dialing for dollars.

For these reasons, concerned groups have promoted the idea of a constitutional amendment to overturn Citizens United, and perhaps to reform other aspects of campaign finance, for instance by leveraging small-dollar contributions with public matching funds, as was described in a bill proposed by Democracy Spring (http://www.democracyspring.org/demands).

* Constitutional amendment

In a number of states (e.g., California, Illinois, and Vermont) there are currently movements to overturn the Citizens United decision via constitutional amendment; an example of an umbrella effort to back this is the Move to Amend campaign (http://www.movetoamend.org/). Their goal is an amendment that would explicitly distinguish between corporations and human beings, and would clarify that money does not qualify as protected free speech, and thus can be regulated by legislation. This process is difficult, requiring 3/4 of the states and 2/3 of both houses of Congress to concur – yet, the Constitution has been amended 27 times, including 17 since the 10 amendments comprising the Bill of Rights were ratified in 1791. Difficult, but possible. And, depending on the final form of the amendment, this could be an important forward step.

* State and local initiatives

While the federal situation is worsening, there have been promising signs within some states. In some cases, there have been state and local initiatives for public funding of campaigns (described in the next section). Additionally, there has been a movement championed by campaign finance thinkers like Trevor Potter and Lawrence Lessig, and by organizations like represent.us, to pass legislation locally (and ultimately at the federal level) called the "American Anti-Corruption Act",[6] which was crafted in 2011 and publicized in 2012. This addresses the campaign finance issue in a very comprehensive way, not only by providing for public financing, but also by handling related potential corruption. For example, such legislation would make it illegal for politicians to accept campaign donations from lobbyists, and would close the "revolving door", in which politicians move from directly from their public positions into high-paying private lobbying jobs. The Act serves as a model for specific legislation to be passed in cities, states, and, ideally, federally. For instance, in 2014, Tallahassee, Florida voters approved a city charter amendment based on this document.

---

[6] http://anticorruptionact.org

3. Public funding of elections

We need to finance our own electoral process.

Since 1976, there has been an option on U.S. federal tax returns to contribute to public funding of presidential election campaigns.

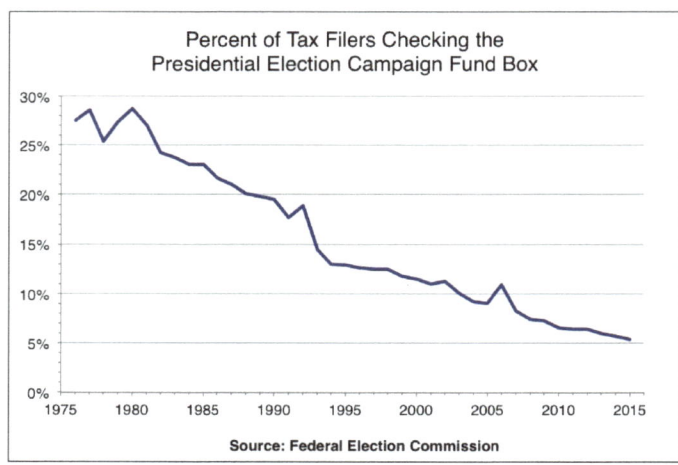

Unfortunately, as shown in the figure below, participation in this optional contribution has steadily declined.

It's not our goal here to argue that this approach is doomed; but clearly, the public has not been supportive of this option through their federal tax returns. Interestingly, on the other hand, a 2013 survey[7] showed 50% support for the idea of public financing in general.

There have been some cases of state and local electoral systems where such approaches have been more successful than public financing at the federal level, and organizations like Every Voice (and its 501(c)(3) spinoff, Every Voice Center) have been working on public funding of elections for a while. For instance, there has recently been progress in Seattle; the "City of Seattle Restrictions on Campaign Finance and Elections, Initiative Measure No. 122" passed in November 2015. Among other provisions, it established a voucher system in which each voter could donate $25 to four candidates of their choice.

In a state-level example, in 1996, Maine passed a popular referendum that encouraged candidates to accept public funding of their campaigns, and to eschew private donations. In Maine (as well as in Arizona and Connecticut, which have similar programs), candidates are eligible for this funding once they have received a specified number of $5 contributions. Such programs are sometimes referred to as "Clean Elections" systems.[8]

However, for recent races, the sums provided were much less than what candidates could receive (and spend) using private funding. In 2015, Maine voters

[7] Lydia Saad, "Half in U.S. Support Publicly Financed Federal Campaigns", Gallup, http://www.gallup.com/poll/163208/half-support-publicly-financed-federal-campaigns.aspx.
[8] See everyvoicecenter.org for more information on these programs.

significantly increased the amount of public funds that could be allocated (and at the same time added new transparency requirements). But the public funding may still be significantly less than what candidates can gather privately. For instance, in Maine's 1st congressional district, as of the March 31 reporting period, the Democratic candidate for the House had received $309,562 in campaign funds from private donors, far more than the $16,500 that would be provided by public funding. The best-funded Republican candidate had received $111,280 from private donors, which still would have been much more than the Democratic candidate would have received using public funding. As long as the costs for a campaign are high (currently the case, but which we want to change), public funding would need to provide much more to candidates to be competitive with the private approach.

In Arizona, campaign finance reform advocates promoted a potential solution for this imbalance, in the Arizona Clean Elections Act, which was passed in 1998. In addition to the funding offered candidates in Maine, according to this Act, publicly funded candidates would receive enough funds to match their privately funded competitors. However, this part of the Act was struck down in a 2011 decision by the U.S. Supreme Court. This decision means that someone turning down public funding can often outmatch the publicly funded candidate. Nonetheless, there are candidates in Arizona, Connecticut, and Maine who have participated in the programs despite their constraints. Such public funding measures may have, at least in some cases at the state and local level, reduced the influence of big money on politics. Indeed, having the public "own" the elections is undoubtedly extremely important.

However, we and many others have observed significant limitations to this approach:

1) As long as the costs of campaigning remain high, due to the competitive need to pay for broadcast ads, staffing, consultants, etc., candidates with deep-pocketed supporters will continue to seek funds from private sources. Ultimately, they will outspend those using only public funding, even where it is available.

2) The most obvious limitation is that these statutes cannot control spending on federal elections.

Despite these limitations, it is our view that public participation in the funding of elections, whether it is via vouchers, broad government funding, or even the type of voluntary contributions from small donors currently seen in many campaigns, is a desirable and important component of the electoral system of the future. But such approaches are unlikely to succeed on their own. In particular, as we said above, as long as the **costs** of running an effective campaign are high (and ever getting higher), money will continue to rule.

We need transparency. We need legal reform, we need to step up and fund our own campaigns. But for these approaches to be successful, we also need to change the way we spend campaign money.

Do the costs have to be so high?

If we only look at past and current practice, yes, it appears they do. Campaigns appear to require an emphasis on expensive mechanisms like television advertising, and experienced political consultants continue to underline their importance. But what if the costs of an effective campaign could be so low that it would seem foolish to spend far more? What if there was a different approach for the future?

That different approach is the topic of the rest of this book.

Part III. A New Way

Don't follow leaders, watch the parking meters.
– Robert Allen Zimmerman (a.k.a. Bob Dylan)

1. Supply and demand

If we can't stop the money from coming in, what can we do?

Campaign finance reformers have been stymied for decades, and the situation has only gotten worse. Reform advocates rightly point to the overwhelming influence of corporations and wealthy individuals as a consequence of the current system, while legal opinions have frequently moved in the direction of interpreting money as speech[9]. This interpretation has led to a significant increase in the influence of major donors on our politics. And arguably, many of the successful reforms that have remained in place have only distributed the corruption in

---

[9] Even as early as in the Buckley v. Valeo decision (1976), the majority opinion noted "A restriction on the amount of money a person or group can spend on political communication during a campaign necessarily reduces the quantity of expression by restricting the number of issues discussed, the depth of their exploration, and the size of the audience reached."

different ways. For instance, the restrictions on contributions to candidates have strengthened the hand of outside groups through Super PACs; the amount of campaign funds spent by Super PACs can often even be higher than what is spent by the campaign committees themselves.

As we noted earlier, the main goal of campaign finance reform has been to limit the supply of money going into the political process, and so far this has been spectacularly unsuccessful. But **what about reducing the demand?**

Suppose, in a future America, there were ways for candidates to accomplish all that they do now, but with a greatly reduced cost? Past a certain point in spending on big-ticket items like TV ads, they provide diminishing returns (for instance, once a candidate has significant name recognition and is associated with some popular idea), and any positive effects tend to wear off within two weeks.[10] But if the cost of effective campaigns was much lower, there would be a different attitude towards fundraising. If a candidate could have more impact by communicating to the public than by phoning donors, many would spend less time on the latter.

In other words, if we can't effectively limit the **supply**, let's reduce the **demand**.

How can we do this? As pointed out in Part I, most campaign expenditures are related to media buys, and television still dominates this cost. Particularly in competitive races, television broadcast time is

---

[10] http://www.psychologyinaction.org/2011/05/27/how-effective-are-political-campaign-advertisements/

very expensive. Many have pointed to using social media as a way to reduce costs, and indeed digital approaches have increased significantly in popularity. It is more straightforward to target relevant populations with digital ads, and there is also a lower threshold on the minimum cost to have an effect – and low-budget campaigns cannot afford to buy many television ads.

However, so far, social media has not demonstrated any obvious advantage over standard broadcast approaches to getting the message out. Typically, even on the Internet, the money is still being spent on ads, often as "pre-roll" (which you see before the content you've clicked on that you actually want). And as the Internet has rapidly become the source of everything, from things of great value to unadulterated garbage, it is difficult to separate the wheat from the chaff.

Both broadcast and digital advertising provide an extremely indirect way of connecting to people (both for influencing persuadable voters and for getting out the vote). It has been shown clearly[11] that word of mouth, particularly from so-called "influencers" to their friends and acquaintances, is by far the most effective approach. So these electronic means should primarily be seen as ways to contact these influencers. But what if campaigns could connect to influencers directly? What if there were low-cost ways to do this, and to organize other campaign functions, so that the high-spending

---

[11] "Finally, Proof That Word of Mouth Isn't Just 'Nice to Have', but Drives Measurable ROI", Ed Keller, Keller Fay (blog), 12/7/2012, http://bit.ly/1VRZS3P.

candidates would just look foolish (as was the case with Jeb Bush's 2016 presidential campaign)?

In the next section, we introduce an approach to highly effective low-cost campaigns, which we believe could ultimately reduce the need for politicians to incessantly beg for money.

2. Power to the People

We can empower peer-to-peer campaigning.

As we said earlier, for campaigns at the federal level (and also for campaigns of significant size within states), the lion's share of the expense is due to advertising, primarily for television. It's not at all clear that this is a very effective way to contact voters, particularly with our increased ability to avoid commercials. A recent study[12] even showed

---

[12] Liam C Malloy and Shanna Pearson-Merkowitz, "Going Positive: The Effects of Negative and Positive Advertising on Candidate Success and Voter Turnout", *Research and Politics* 3, no.1 (2016), DOI 10.1177/2053168015625078.

that a spending advantage applied to negative ads tends to **decrease** support for the attacker.

Nonetheless, candidates require name recognition, and beyond that, few would want to risk being outmatched in any mechanism for promoting their message, including television ads.

But every choice requires tradeoffs. Every dollar spent on TV ads is a dollar that could be spent on something else. Every hour of a candidate's time spent on "dialing for dollars" is an hour that could be spent on direct contact with voters – or for incumbents, actually doing their job. And whether the goal is influencing persuadable voters or Get-Out-the-Vote (GOTV) among a candidate's likely supporters, ultimately what works is enrolling what the advertising world refers to as "influencers", who then pass the message on to people who trust them.

We argued above that putting an ad on TV (or, for that matter, on Facebook) could be seen as a way of reaching these influencers – but it is still a very indirect way. On the other hand, we already have a much more direct mechanism, already in use, but underutilized: political volunteers.

Many people are willing to donate their time in an election. But few candidates maximize the utility of their volunteers. Part of the solution requires a shift in attitude. Currently, campaigns mostly treat volunteers as "cannon fodder" for the conflict, people who can be directed into performing routine tasks as needed (for instance, being handed a rote script to read to people they are directed to call – that is, to those who don't hang up right away). And in many campaigns, volunteers are charged for the swag that used to be free to hand out (like lawn signs), and in fact profits from this are a source of funding for the campaign. This is an extreme case of underutilizing the volunteers – seeing them as a profit source rather than properly equipping them to go out and spread the word.

But volunteers are actually a sample of the general voting population, only with a greater-than-typical interest in the political process. Many of them have skills and experience that can dwarf that of the paid staff. In particular, a fraction of them will have specific high-value professional skills that the campaign needs (such as video production, journalism, or web design), and will be willing to use those skills (if not for free, for cut rates) in the service of a campaign they believe in.

Not every candidate will be able to attract a large cadre of volunteers. A candidate needs to be attractive to volunteers in order to significantly benefit from their efforts. This is a sensible, constraint, one that is analogous to the requirement of amassing small donations to qualify for public funding. But this is far more democratic than the requirement to know enough wealthy individuals.

There is a common perception that harnessing volunteer passion is far too difficult, due to the chaos that is often seen. Fully leveraging volunteer effort will require a systematic use of the right tools to make it straightforward. In some cases, existing general applications can be jury-rigged to provide the required functionality, but the effort can be streamlined by developing methods and tools that are specifically designed for this task. The next section describes what this could look like.

3. The role of technology

Can technology help?

We live in an age of technology hype. Every smart phone innovation is celebrated; every technical advance is hailed as a life-changer. "Head down" has become one of the most popular postures.

It's true that social media has become an inescapable part of our culture – for instance, over a billion people use Facebook on a daily basis. Cameras are everywhere, and in a large number of cities, technology-enabled ridesharing is a reality. Self-driving cars have been demonstrated, and many automated safety features have already been introduced in human-driven cars. And computational power that dwarfs what was found in a top-of-the-line workstation a decade ago is now in our pockets, in the ubiquitous smart phone.

But technology has impact beyond the "wow" factor. Each of the technology-related changes around us (not all of them positive) is associated with some social effects as well. Kentaro Toyama put it well: "Technology's primary effect is to amplify human forces."[13] In other words, while we can't solve social problems with a technological fix, we can use technology as a tool to empower people to tackle and solve social problems. So far at least, the rapid changes in technology have done little to change the political landscape. Despite all the growth in social media, most of the money in large campaigns is still spent on TV ads (or on pre-roll commercials online).

This is not to say that technology is necessarily useless when it comes to democratizing our politics. But it needs to be harnessed in a way that amplifies positive changes in how electoral politics is done. We believe that technology CAN amplify people's ability to engage with their government. In the particular context of this book, technology needs to provide services for political campaigns in a way

---

[13] Kentaro Toyama, *Geek Heresy*, https://itun.es/us/DhDX5.l.

that keeps costs down while significantly improving the efficacy of the electoral effort.

As we will elaborate on in later sections, it is actually somewhat surprising how poorly the current expensive methods (like negative TV ads) work, and how well fairly inexpensive things (driven by volunteer effort) can work. But volunteer efforts are typically undervalued and under-supported. What if technology could be harnessed to make volunteer efforts much more efficient, much more organized, while enhancing volunteers' sense of empowerment? What if offline message communication via word of mouth could be supported and amplified by online organizational tools? This would not require major new technological advances (we're not proposing portable holograms of candidates to be used for canvassing), but really just an emphasis on using the best technology for the volunteer-driven ground game.

Much of the technology for such a shift already exists, in some form or other. Some of the basics that are available to us as system builders in the current environment:

1) Location-based algorithms – between the availability of GPS information and standard graphical visualization approaches, there are a host of methods to track progress in ground-based offline efforts.

2) Scheduling software – it is now straightforward to provide user-friendly

interfaces to organize the activities of large numbers of volunteers.

3) Matching algorithms – there are simple methods that can be immediately deployed to match the skills and experience of volunteers to the needs of campaigns.

Part IV. Why This Will Work

A dream you dream alone is only a dream. A dream you dream together is reality.
– John Lennon

1. The importance of the ground game

Local efforts are the most effective.

For well-funded campaigns, most of the money is spent on television ads. But are they the most effective element? On the other hand, if we are proposing a shift to predominantly offline ground game activities, which are potentially much cheaper, what evidence is there that this would be preferable?

Let's start with the humble lawn sign. How low-tech can you go? Common campaign wisdom would suggest that lawn and window signs are of minor importance – and many campaigns reinforce this view by spending no money on them, depending instead on volunteers to choose to put them up if they are so inclined.

And yet, a recent study[14] based on four randomized field trials showed that, on average, signs increased

---

[14] Donald P. Green, Jonathan S. Krasno, Alexander Coppock, Benjamin D. Farrer, Brandon Lenoir, and Joshua N. Zingher,

vote share by 1.7 percentage points for a variety of campaigns. This is significantly more than what has been observed for TV ads, even when they are positive and the opponent has been significantly outspent.

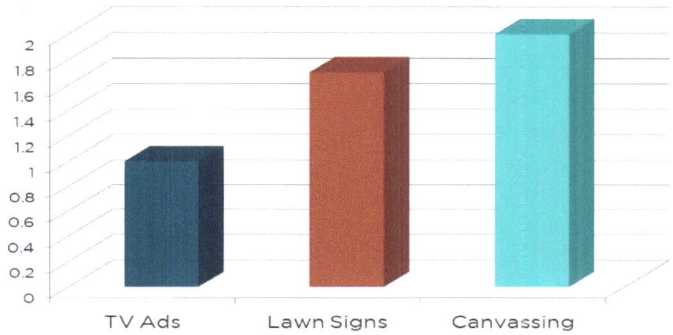

As the figure shows, lawn signs are (on average) almost twice as effective than the far more expensive TV ads[15], and almost as effective as the more labor-intensive canvassing[16].

In fact, direct outreach is the most important factor in influencing election outcomes. For instance, 37% of people say they do not trust TV ads at all, while only 17% don't trust recommendations from

"The Effects of Lawn Signs on Vote Outcomes: Results from Four Randomized Field Experiments", *Electoral Studies* 41 (2016), DOI: 10.1016/j.electstud.2015.12.002.

[15] Liam C Malloy and Shanna Pearson-Merkowitz (2016). Going Positive: The Effects of Negative and Positive Advertising on Candidate Success and Voter Turnout. Research and Politics, January-March 2016

[16] Vincent Pons (2016). *Will a Five-Minute Discussion Change Your Mind? A Countrywide Experiment on Voter Choice in France*. Harvard Business School Working Paper, No. 16-079, January 2016

"people we know and trust".[17] Arguably, even the way broadcast ads work (when they do), is by affecting political "influencers"; advertisers know this, and typically design ads to reach influencers. These individuals speak with their friends and co-workers, who know they are hearing from someone who is more involved in the topic of the ad, which in our case is politics – much as people rely on people in their personal networks to get restaurant recommendations.

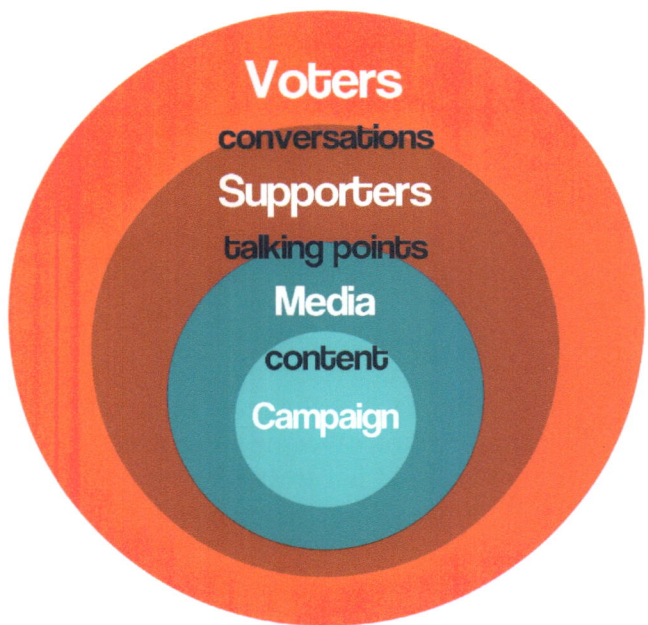

If this is how the campaign message is really spread, and if expensive TV ads are an inefficient way to do it, why not use more direct means to

[17] Neilsen, "Global Trust in Advertising: Winning Strategies for an Evolving Media Landscape", September 2015, http://bit.ly/1Plj03A.

make it happen? There are powerful economic incentives in place to use the inefficient approaches, in particular for political consultants who make significant profits from the emphasis on major media buys; this can consciously or unconsciously bias their recommendations.

This is why our new organization, UpRise Campaigns, emphasizes the ground game, focusing on energized volunteers who can spread the message. Our goal is to empower these volunteers, not only with useful technology, but also with the sense that their unique capabilities are being recognized.

Of course, the notion of a "ground game" is not new; many campaigns at least have a ground component. And it's true that even recent campaigns that have really emphasized the ground game have not always been successful. But why is that?

2. What's been missing in grassroots electoral approaches

We can organize the chaos of volunteers and win elections.

As we pointed out earlier, well-funded campaigns have increasingly relied on expensive media distribution to reach the public with their message. But if less expensive "ground game" approaches are more effective, why don't low-resource campaigns (those that lack the funds to use expensive media approaches) win more often?

Certainly we can point to examples where a campaign with fewer resources has done well, and in particular has done better than well-funded opponents. But these are the exception rather than the rule. Why is this, given the evidence for the greater effectiveness of cheaper methods?

In a nutshell, the answer is this: **organization!** It is one thing to profess the utility of the ground game, but quite another to structure it in a way that will be effective. Most campaigns only have a few paid staff in an area, including an underpaid and overworked volunteer coordinator trying their best to manage the random people that walk through their door. Ground-based techniques that are based on large campaign staffs are still quite expensive, while reliance on volunteers without adequate support can lead to chaos. And just using many volunteers is no recipe for success – if their experience and abilities are not recognized, then their contributions may still have minimal value, and potentially be dispiriting for them. Imagine for instance an experienced copywriter who is relegated to reading a prepackaged script on randomly selected phone calls.

Aside from the lack of a proper skills matching system for volunteers, campaigns have a limited ability to schedule volunteer efforts in a way that takes advantage of voter information and that avoids under- or over-coverage of particular physical areas. While micro-targeting approaches have become quite sophisticated, particularly for large campaigns (e.g., presidential), down-ballot races have limited abilities to schedule the best volunteer effort at the best time and place. In short, we lack ubiquitous and convenient tools for this purpose. The result is often a mess, where thousands of left hands don't know what thousands of right hands are doing.

3. What needs to happen: UpRise Campaigns

Where do we go from here?

UpRise Campaigns has been formed to develop systems and training approaches to organize and empower volunteers. With the right tools, the volunteer effort can be made far more effective, and thus an inexpensive component can become the dominant part of campaigns. Our tools will facilitate direct outreach to voters, adapting effective word-of-mouth marketing tactics to the unique domain of political campaigns. This will achieve the goal of significantly reducing the cost of campaigns, and thus disrupt the need to raise so much money. It will also help to develop an organized, engaged citizenry over the long term. You can visit uprisecampaigns.org to see more about the types of activities and events we are working to organize.

What needs to happen next? UpRise needs to reach large numbers of concerned citizens and spread these ideas, to turn our effort into a movement. We have seen political movements with great enthusiasm for decades, often associated with electoral campaigns – most recently Obama 2008 and Sanders 2016. Both of these campaigns tapped into the energy of many volunteers. However, there was no single campaign that established a persistent structure and set of organizing ideas that could build on the enthusiasm for those particular candidates and take it one step further, to help those volunteers stay involved across a wide range of campaigns. This structure is what we are working to build, but it will require the participation of a critical mass of potential volunteers and supporters of the ideas.

Some of this structure is based on tools that we are building, but also it will involve training, coalition building, and the creation of a movement based on these ideas.

That is where we need to go next, and you, the reader, can be the foundation of such a structure. When we reach critical mass, we will be able to change the way campaigns work, and will be well on our way to eliminating the "soft" corruption of big money in politics (corruption that is not illegal, but which is still harmful). Lowering the cost and raising the efficacy of campaigns will complement the other approaches to this issue, such as anti-corruption legislation and public financing.

You have already begun by reading this book –
now, go to uprisecampaigns.org and become a
member. Welcome to the team!

Epilogue: A Personal Note[18]

The work described here results from the combined efforts of the UpRise founders. Antonia Scatton has worked on campaigns for decades, and developed the core ideas around volunteer empowerment. Barath Raghavan's experience as a volunteer on the 2008 Obama campaign influenced his ideas of what worked well in that effort, and his research on Internet security and on community-oriented technology initiatives has influenced the technical approaches we are implementing. Madelaine Plauché's experience in designing user interfaces that facilitate citizen engagement in domains of government, education, and health has been crucial in developing technology that volunteers can actually use.

Many of the ideas expressed here arise out of Scatton's political campaign experiences. She saw both the potential of volunteer efforts and the *wasted* potential of how volunteers were often employed in practice. Over time, she developed a set of ideas for the effective use of volunteer efforts in election campaigns.

Scatton also was strongly influenced by the work of cognitive linguist George Lakoff, with whom she worked for an extended period. Lakoff clarified for her some of the processes that affect elections; among other things, he affirmed the vital importance of understanding and expressing values in the effective communication of a candidate's message.

---

[18] By the eldest co-author (that would be Morgan).

In late 2014, Scatton and I met; along with my colleague Raghavan, I was exploring ways to reduce the cost of political campaigns (in order to reduce the demand for large donations). Scatton's ideas were really the complement of my own, and it was clear that we should work together. This was formalized (after also bringing in Plauché) by the formation of UpRise Campaigns in June 2015. UpRise is what's called a "Social Purpose Corporation", which is a kind of organization under California law that places a particular social purpose over profit. This was chosen over a purely not-for-profit structure so that UpRise could coordinate directly with electoral campaigns, which a non-profit cannot do.

A successful crowdfunding campaign in late 2015 provided us with enough funds to build a basic code base to provide structure to a number of key volunteer activities, and to clarify our message and begin talking to campaign personnel who could be potential users of our tools and approach.

I was fortunate to be able to bring together these phenomenal people, as well as an exceptional set of advisors, such as Lakoff, as well as Robert Reich. The main story described here was developed as a group, and the emphasis should be on that story, and not on any individual. But I do want to add a bit about how I got to this place.

My own professional career has been pretty distant from politics; for the last few decades, I've worked on technology for machine recognition of speech (the sort of thing that "Siri" does), and on trying to understand how the human brain does this. I also worked in a branch of artificial intelligence called "neural networks", in which large connected groups of simple computational elements can perform quite sophisticated classifications and predictions. Probably most relevant to the needs of UpRise Campaigns, I spent over a decade as the director of the International Computer Science Institute, a research center closely affiliated with the University of California at Berkeley. This provided me with management experience that I definitely needed to launch an organization like UpRise Campaigns.

So what led me to the UpRise mission? Well, part of it is negative – I've worked in technology for 40 years, and its effects are almost always double-edged. Technology does good things, and sometimes, not so much. Often it changes things for good and ill at the same time.

So after all this time, I wanted to do something that was unequivocally good. Maybe there's no such thing – but there are many efforts one could make that would overwhelmingly be positive. So many that it can be hard to choose. Work with an environmental organization? An anti-war group? Lobby for universal preschool? Etc.

What turned me towards the UpRise Campaigns route was the realization that progress on just about any issue one could imagine was stalled in this country by a dysfunctional political system. Even things that seem obvious (how about replacing crumbling infrastructure before it gets even more expensive to fix?) are seemingly impossible to move on. And the more I looked at it, the more it seemed like the influence of big money in the process was a prime cause of this paralysis. Disrupting it seemed like it was not only an unadulterated good, but also could have the broadest effect in addressing a host of evils in our society. So in 2014, I began to cut back on my purely technological and scientific efforts to focus on this problem.

Although this was a complete departure for my professional career, in some ways it was a return to my roots. I was always concerned with the political system, as a bystander, to be sure, but nonetheless as one who paid attention. I was a donor to progressive candidates and causes, and particularly focused on the process, both for the Obama 2008 campaign and for Barbara Boxer's Senate campaigns. But more fundamentally, I began with an idealistic focus before I became an adult. My parents were socialists; my uncle Manny was blacklisted for decades (for telling the House Un-American Activities Committee what they could do with their unconstitutional interrogation), and as a teenager I demonstrated against the Vietnam War. The revolution didn't quite happen, but the obvious value of trying to save the world in one way or another stayed with me.

This new effort has returned me to a version of my younger focus – but now I think of it as working to making this a better country for my grandchildren and beyond. Together with my UpRise partners, I'm determined to change how things are done, no matter how long it takes. This can't be done by one person, or by our four founders alone, but I believe that we can help. And if you have read this far, maybe you are going to be part of this change. I really hope so.

For Further Reading

Ansolabehere, Stephen, & Iyengar, Shanto. (1995). *Going negative: How attack ads shrink and polarize the electorate*. New York: Free Press.

Keller, Ed, & Fay, Brad. (2012). *The face-to-face book: Why real relationships rule in a digital marketplace*. New York: Free Press.

Lakoff, George. (2004). *Don't think of an elephant! Know your values and frame the debate: The essential guide for progressives*. White River Junction, VT: Chelsea Green.

Lessig, Lawrence. (2014). *The USA is Lesterland: The nature of congressional corruption*.

Putnam, Robert D. (2000). *Bowling alone: The collapse and revival of American community*. New York: Simon & Schuster.

Toyama, Kentaro. (2015). *Geek heresy. Rescuing social change from the cult of technology*. New York: PublicAffairs. Available from iBooks: https://itun.es/us/DhDX5.l.

And of course, go to

UpRiseCampaigns.org

for updates on our activities (and to support this idea by becoming a member).

Image Credits

Front cover: "The Giant Corruption Machine" by Clay Butler for UpRise Campaigns.

Part I

Page 1: "Robot TV Attack" by Clay Butler for UpRise Campaigns; modified by the authors.

Page 2: "Presidential Campaigns, Total Cost in Millions" by Antonia Scatton for UpRise Campaigns; based on data from the Center for Responsive Politics, https://www.opensecrets.org.

Page 3: "Tillis Vote Tweet" by the authors (screenshot).

Page 4: Supreme Court front image via Pixabay https://pixabay.com/en/supreme-court-building-usa-546279/, Creative Commons license 0 (public domain).

Page 7: Moneybag (untitled) by OpenClipartVectors via Pixabay, https://pixabay.com/en/bag-dollar-hoard-money-moneybag-1299303/, Creative Commons license 0 (public domain).

Page 8: "Poor Musician One Legged" by OCAL via ClipShrine, http://www.clipshrine.com/Poor-Musician-One-Legged-17776-medium.html, Creative Commons license 0 (public domain).

Page 10: "Where Does the Money Go?" by Antonia Scatton for UpRise Campaigns; based on data from the Center for Responsive Politics, https://www.opensecrets.org.

Page 11: Merry-go-round (untitled) by Dean Moriarty via Pixabay, https://pixabay.com/en/merry-go-round-fair-fun-1293509/, Creative Commons license 0 (public domain).

Page 12: Money changing hands (untitled) by ClkerFreeVectorImages via Pixabay, https://pixabay.com/en/money-hand-people-hands-currency-38268/, Creative Commons license 0 (public domain).

Part II

Page 15: "Wrong Address" © the Everett Collection via Shutterstock, http://www.shutterstock.com/pic-227272540/stock-photo-wrong-address.html.

Page 16: Light shining in the darkness (untitled) by Gerd Altmann via Pixabay, https://pixabay.com/en/background-spotlight-light-rays-767926/, Creative Commons license 0 (public domain).

Page 19: "Dictionary Definition of the Word Legislation in English [with] Vignetting Effect" © Roman Motizov via Shutterstock, http://www.shutterstock.com/pic-395553598/stock-photo-dictionary-definition-of-the-word-legislation-in-english-vignetting-effect.html.

Page 22: Image from 1040 form, followed by "Percent of Tax Filers Checking the Presidential Election Campaign Fund Box" by the authors; based on data from the Federal Election Commission, http://www.fec.gov.

Part III

Page 27: Hands of people working together, © hxdbzxy via shutterstock, http://www.shutterstock.com/pic-166555364/stock-photo-people-with-their-hands-together-team-work-concept.html?src=J7fuSHbOMpFiQJy_tStVhw-1-4

Page 28: Buy/sell (untitled) by Gerd Altmann via Pixabay, https://pixabay.com/en/dollar-businessman-finance-buy-789114/, Creative Commons license 0 (public domain).

Page 32: World democracy (untitled) by Gerd Altmann via Pixabay, https://pixabay.com/en/demokratie-people-power-450597/, Creative Commons license 0 (public domain).

Page 35: Robot with flower (untitled) by bamenny via Pixabay, https://pixabay.com/en/robot-flower-technology-future-1214536/, Creative Commons license 0 (public domain).

Page 35: Dinner guests looking down at cell phones © iko via Shutterstock, http://www.shutterstock.com/pic-306965114

Part IV

Page 39 (and back cover): Rosie the Riveter poster (untitled image), reproduction by PublicDomainPictures via Pixabay, https://pixabay.com/en/poster-vintage-antique-war-316690/, Creative Commons license 0 (public domain).

Page 40: "American Football Player in Action with Ball" © Pete Saloutos via Shutterstock, http://www.shutterstock.com/pic-43949293/stock-photo-american-football-player-in-action-with-ball.html.

Page 41: "Effects of Campaign Elements on Election Outcomes" by Antonia Scatton for UpRise Campaigns, using data from publications in footnotes 14, 15, and 16.

Page 42: "How Influencers Spread the Message" by Antonia Scatton for UpRise Campaigns.

Page 44: "Young Man in Cable Chaos with Wrong Plugs" © Camilo Torres via Shutterstock, http://www.shutterstock.com/pic-15348133/stock-photo-young-man-in-cable-chaos-with- wrong-plugs.html.

Page 46: "The One Thing Money Can't Buy" by Clay Butler for UpRise Campaigns; modified by the authors.